THE LOS ANGELES RAMS

BY JANIE SCHEFFER

A NFL TEAM

EPIC

BELLWETHER MEDIA ★ MINNEAPOLIS, MN

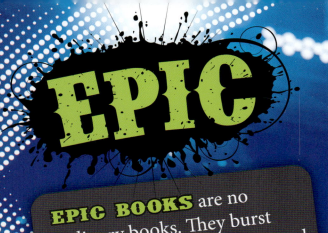

EPIC BOOKS are no ordinary books. They burst with intense action, high-speed heroics, and shadows of the unknown. Are you ready for an Epic adventure?

This book is intended for educational use. Organization and franchise logos are trademarks of the National Football League (NFL). This is not an official book of the NFL. It is not approved by or connected with the NFL.

This edition first published in 2024 by Bellwether Media, Inc.

No part of this publication may be reproduced in whole or in part without written permission of the publisher. For information regarding permission, write to Bellwether Media, Inc., Attention: Permissions Department, 6012 Blue Circle Drive, Minnetonka, MN 55343.

Library of Congress Cataloging-in-Publication Data

Names: Scheffer, Janie, 1992- author.
Title: The Los Angeles Rams / by Janie Scheffer.
Description: Minneapolis, MN : Bellwether Media, 2024. | Series: Epic. NFL team profiles | Includes bibliographical references and index. | Audience: Ages 7-12 | Audience: Grades 2-3 | Summary: "Engaging images accompany information about the Los Angeles Rams. The combination of high-interest subject matter and light text is intended for students in grades 2 through 7"-- Provided by publisher.
Identifiers: LCCN 2023021994 (print) | LCCN 2023021995 (ebook) | ISBN 9798886874846 (library binding) | ISBN 9798886876727 (ebook)
Subjects: LCSH: Los Angeles Rams (Football team : 2016-)--History--Juvenile literature. | St. Louis Rams (Football team)--History--Juvenile literature. | Los Angeles Rams (Football team : 1946-1994)--History--Juvenile literature.
Classification: LCC GV956.L6 S35 2024 (print) | LCC GV956.L6 (ebook) | DDC 796.332/640979494--dc23/eng/20230515
LC record available at https://lccn.loc.gov/2023021994
LC ebook record available at https://lccn.loc.gov/2023021995

Text copyright © 2024 by Bellwether Media, Inc. EPIC and associated logos are trademarks and/or registered trademarks of Bellwether Media, Inc.

Editor: Kieran Downs   Designer: Josh Brink

Printed in the United States of America, North Mankato, MN.

TABLE OF CONTENTS

STAFFORD TO KUPP	4
THE HISTORY OF THE RAMS	6
THE RAMS TODAY	14
GAME DAY!	16
LOS ANGELES RAMS FACTS	20
GLOSSARY	22
TO LEARN MORE	23
INDEX	24

STAFFORD TO KUPP

MATTHEW STAFFORD

The Rams are playing in **Super Bowl** 56. Less than 2 minutes are left in the game. The Bengals are winning 20–16.

Rams **quarterback** Matthew Stafford throws a pass. **Wide receiver** Cooper Kupp catches it. **Touchdown**! The Rams go on to win!

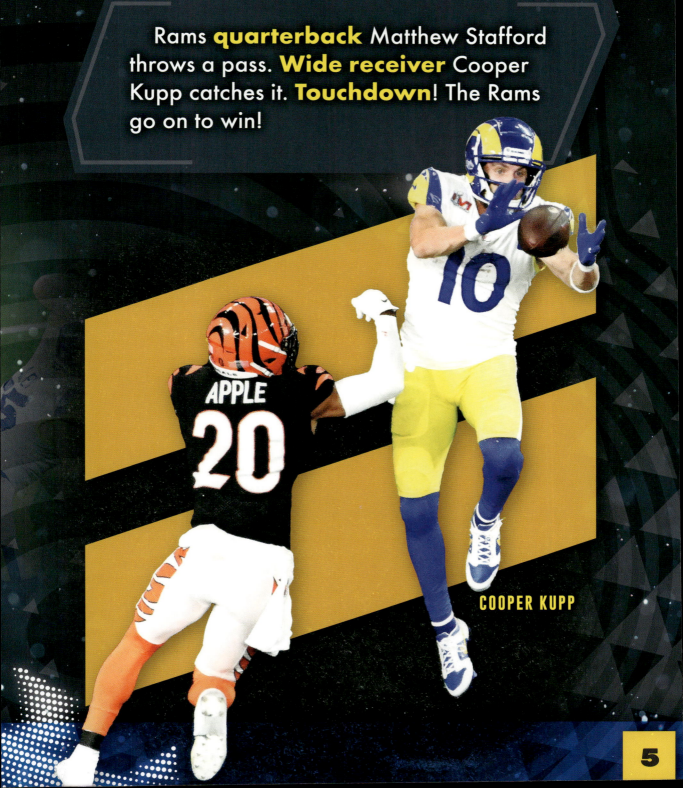

COOPER KUPP

5

THE HISTORY OF THE RAMS

The Rams began in Cleveland, Ohio, in 1936. The next year, they joined the National Football League (NFL). In 1945, they won the NFL **championship**.

In 1946, the Rams moved to Los Angeles, California. The team won another championship in 1951.

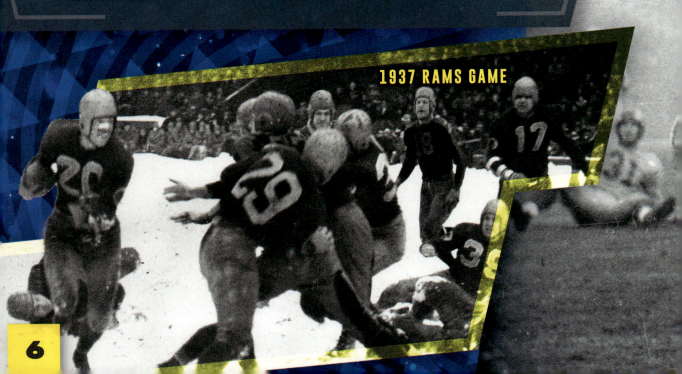

1937 RAMS GAME

1949 RAMS GAME

HELMET DECORATIONS

The Rams put decorations on their helmets in 1948. They were the first team to do so.

7

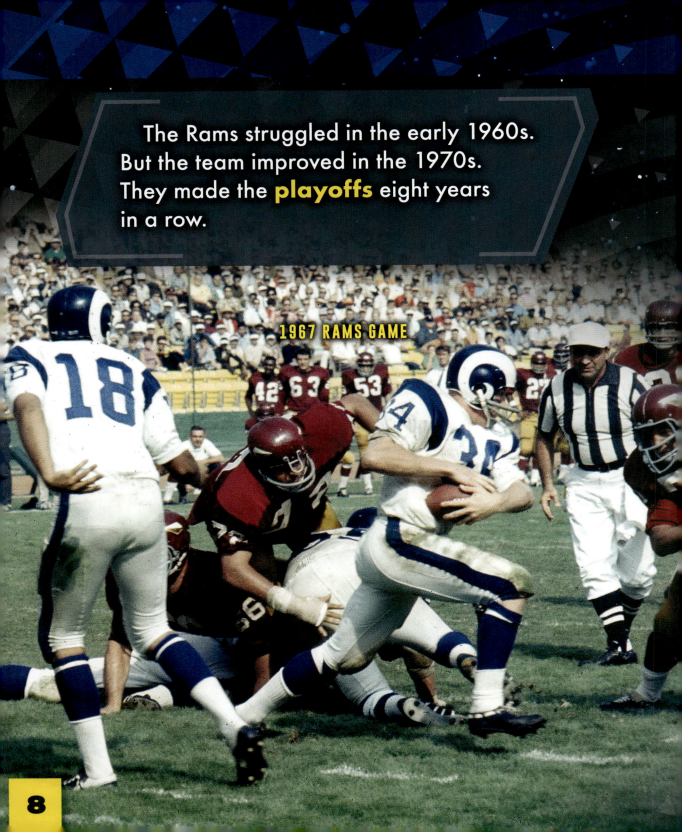

The Rams struggled in the early 1960s. But the team improved in the 1970s. They made the **playoffs** eight years in a row.

1967 RAMS GAME

SUPER BOWL 14

In 1980, the Rams played in Super Bowl 14. But they lost to the Pittsburgh Steelers.

The Rams were a strong running team in the 1980s. They were led by **running back** Eric Dickerson.

ERIC DICKERSON

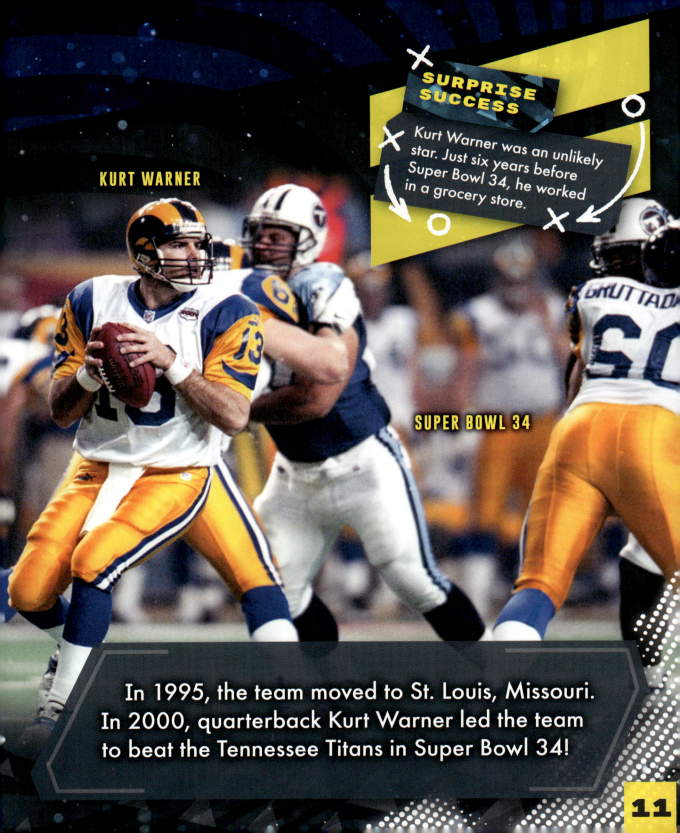

KURT WARNER

SURPRISE SUCCESS

Kurt Warner was an unlikely star. Just six years before Super Bowl 34, he worked in a grocery store.

SUPER BOWL 34

In 1995, the team moved to St. Louis, Missouri. In 2000, quarterback Kurt Warner led the team to beat the Tennessee Titans in Super Bowl 34!

In 2002, the Rams lost to the New England Patriots in Super Bowl 36. In 2016, the team moved back to Los Angeles.

SUPER BOWL 56

HEADED HOME

Super Bowl 56 was played at SoFi Stadium. The Rams were the second team to play a Super Bowl game at home.

12

The Rams lost again in Super Bowl 53. But they beat the Cincinnati Bengals in Super Bowl 56!

TROPHY CASE

SUPER BOWL championships: 2

NFL championships: 2

NFC WEST championships: 14

NFC championships: 5

THE RAMS TODAY

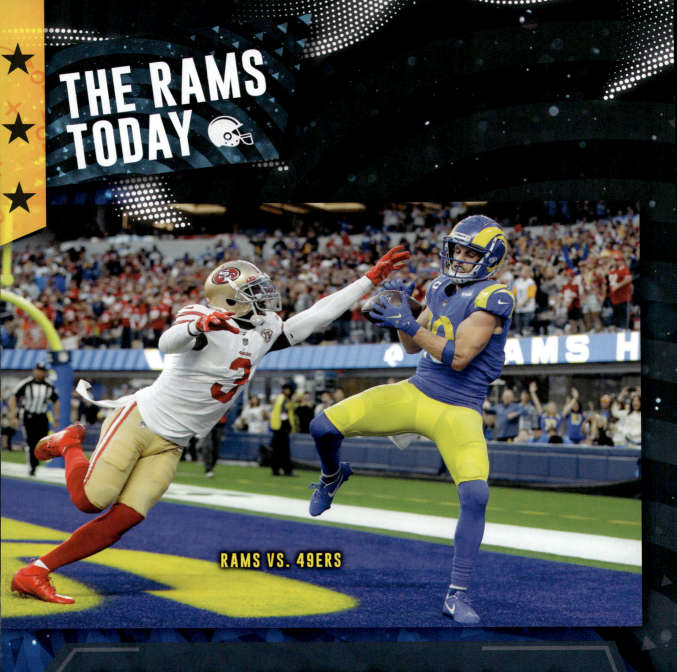

RAMS VS. 49ERS

The Rams play at SoFi **Stadium** in Inglewood, California. It opened in 2020.

The team is part of the NFC West. The Rams' biggest **rival** is the San Francisco 49ers.

📍 LOCATION 📍

CALIFORNIA

SoFi STADIUM
Inglewood, California

15

GAME DAY!

The Rams track which uniforms are worn during winning games. They wear the lucky ones again!

Rampage is the team's **mascot**. He wears blue and yellow. These are the team's colors.

BIG HOME

SoFi Stadium's site is huge. It is over three times bigger than Disneyland!

SOFI STADIUM

RAMPAGE

The **Mariachi** Rams play music at home games to pump up the team and fans. Some fans wear watermelons on their heads. They proudly yell "Whose House? Rams' House!"

The Rams' house has moved a few times. But the fans have always followed!

MARIACHI RAMS

★ FAMOUS PLAYERS ★

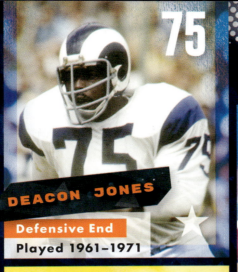

75

DEACON JONES
Defensive End
Played 1961–1971

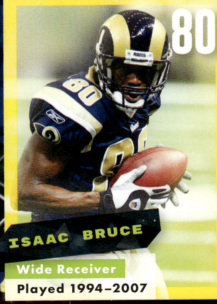

80

ISAAC BRUCE
Wide Receiver
Played 1994–2007

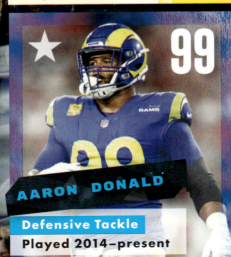

99

AARON DONALD
Defensive Tackle
Played 2014–present

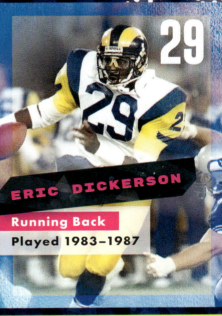

29

ERIC DICKERSON
Running Back
Played 1983–1987

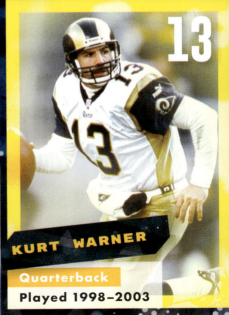

13

KURT WARNER
Quarterback
Played 1998–2003

19

LOS ANGELES RAMS FACTS

LOGO

JOINED THE NFL	1937

MASCOT

RAMPAGE

NICKNAMES	None

CONFERENCE

National Football Conference (NFC)

COLORS

DIVISION | NFC West

 Arizona Cardinals

 San Francisco 49ers

 Seattle Seahawks

STADIUM

★ SoFi STADIUM ★

opened September 8, 2020

holds **70,240** people

20

🕐 TIMELINE

1936
The Rams begin in Cleveland

1946
The Rams move to Los Angeles

2000
The Rams win Super Bowl 34

2016
The Rams move back to Los Angeles from St. Louis

2022
The Rams win Super Bowl 56 at home

★ RECORDS ★

| All-Time Passing Leader | All-Time Rushing Leader | All-Time Receiving Leader | All-Time Scoring Leader |

Jim Everett
23,758 yards

Steven Jackson
10,138 yards

Isaac Bruce
14,109 yards

Jeff Wilkins
1,223 points

GLOSSARY

championship—a contest to decide the best team or person

mariachi—related to a type of Mexican folk music performed by costumed musicians who move while playing

mascot—an animal or symbol that represents a sports team

playoffs—games played after the regular season is over; playoff games determine which teams play in the championship game.

quarterback—a player whose main job is to throw and hand off the ball

rival—a long-standing opponent

running back—a player whose main job is to run with the ball

stadium—an arena where sports are played

Super Bowl—the annual championship game of the NFL

touchdown—a score that occurs when a team crosses into their opponent's end zone with the football; a touchdown is worth six points.

wide receiver—a player whose main job is to catch passes from the quarterback

TO LEARN MORE

AT THE LIBRARY

Coleman, Ted. *Los Angeles Rams All-Time Greats*. Mendota Heights, Minn.: Press Box Books, 2022.

Rice, Dona. *Ride with Rampage*. Aliso Viejo, Calif.: Michaelson Entertainment, 2021.

Whiting, Jim. *Los Angeles Rams*. Mankato, Minn.: Creative Education, 2019.

ON THE WEB

FACTSURFER

Factsurfer.com gives you a safe, fun way to find more information.

1. Go to www.factsurfer.com.

2. Enter "Los Angeles Rams" into the search box and click 🔍.

3. Select your book cover to see a list of related content.

INDEX

Cleveland, Ohio, 6
colors, 16, 20
Dickerson, Eric, 10
famous players, 19
fans, 18
history, 4, 5, 6, 7, 8, 9, 10, 11, 12, 13, 14
Inglewood, California, 14, 15
Kupp, Cooper, 5
Los Angeles, California, 6, 12
Los Angeles Rams facts, 20–21
Mariachi Rams, 18
mascot, 16, 17, 20
National Football League (NFL), 6, 20
NFC West, 15, 20
NFL championship, 6
playoffs, 8
positions, 5, 10, 11
records, 21
rival, 15
SoFi Stadium, 12, 14, 15, 17, 20
St. Louis, Missouri, 11
Stafford, Matthew, 4, 5
Super Bowl, 4, 5, 9, 11, 12, 13
timeline, 21
trophy case, 13
uniforms, 7, 16
Warner, Kurt, 11

The images in this book are reproduced through the courtesy of: Kevin Sabitus/ AP Images, cover; Eric Glenn, cover (stadium); UPI/ Alamy, pp. 2-3, 18 (watermelon headed fans); Michael Owens/ Getty Images, pp. 4-5, 14, 21 (timeline 2022); MediaNews Group/ Los Angeles Daily News via Getty Images/ Getty Images, p. 5; ASSOCIATED PRESS/ AP Images, pp. 6, 21 (timeline 1946); Vic Stein/ Getty Images, pp. 6-7, 8-9; Peter Read Miller/ Getty Images, p. 9; George Gojkovich/ Getty Images, p. 10; Al Messerschmidt, AP Images, p. 11; Ronald Martinez/ Getty Images, pp. 12-13; stellalevi, p. 15 (stadium); Los Angeles Rams/ Wikipedia, pp. 15 (Rams Logo), 20 (Rams logo); Ben Liebenberg/ AP Images, pp. 16, 16-17, 20 (mascot); John McCoy/ Getty Images, pp. 18-19; Focus On Sport/ Getty Images, p. 19 (Deacon Jones); Lennox McLendon/ AP Images, p. 19 (Eric Dickerson); Bill Greenblatt/ Alamy, p. 19 (Isaac Bruce); Allen Kee/ AP Newsroom, p. 19 (Kurt Warner); MediaNews Group/ Pasadena Star-News via Getty Images/ Getty Images, p. 19 (Aaron Donald); NFL Enterprises LLC./ Wikipedia, p. 20 (conference); Arizona Cardinals/ Wikipedia, p. 20 (Cardinals logo); 49ers/ Wikipedia, p. 20 (49ers logo); Seahawks/ Wikipedia, p. 20 (Seahawks logo); Diane Modafferi/ Alamy, p. 20 (stadium); Vuelo Aerial Media, p. 21 (timeline 1936); Andy Kuno/ Alamy, p. 21 (timeline 2000); ActionPlus Sports Images/ Alamy, p. 21 (timeline 2016); Paul Popper/ Popperfoto, Getty Images, p. 21 (Jim Everett); David Welker/ Getty Images, p. 21 (Steven Jackson); Sporting News Archive/ Getty Images, p. 21 (Isaac Bruce); Elsa/ Getty Images, p. 21 (Jeff Wilkins); All-Pro Reels/ Wikipedia, p. 23.